To Lore
with love

Suzi Wilks
xxx

ARE YOU EMOTIONALLY AVAILABLE?

Gorgeous Johnny

love

you

Debs xxx

BLUE ANGEL
PUBLISHING

Foreword

The book you have in your hands is a gem. It is a generous gift from two remarkable women. Suzie and Deborah have courageously confronted their own life experiences and distilled from them some essential truths which encourage and assist all of us. This small book sparkles with wit as well as wisdom. We could not wish for more delightful companions or a more useful guide on our own, sometimes perplexing and even painful journey.

Punch the word "loneliness" into Google and you will find thirteen million five hundred thousand entries. As a psychotherapist, I am daily confronting the wounded suffering the bewilderment and pain of a broken relationship, those suffering rejection, loneliness, those questioning their own worth, wondering if a nurturing love relationship will ever be theirs.

I believe in "bibliotherapy." By that I mean that my clients are accustomed to my offering them books which I think will be helpful to them in resolving their problem. We are all involved in the ongoing work of creating ourselves. Often, it is in the pages of a book, even a single new insight found in a book, that we get the "breakthrough" that reveals us to ourselves or the "turnaround" which removes a sometimes self-imposed barrier to our achieving our goals.

This book is one of those I am going to have on my "prescription" list, and I am certain I will not be the only one to celebrate its value in helping us achieve our most heartfelt goals.

Clayton C. Barbeau, M.A., MFT

International best-selling author of "Delivering the Male," and "Joy of Marriage."

RU EA?

Published in 2009 by Blue Angel Publishing
80 Glen Tower Drive, Glen Waverley
Victoria, Australia 3150
Phone: +61 3 9574 7776
Fax: +61 3 9574 7772
E-mail: tonicarmine@optusnet.com.au
Website: www.blueangelonline.com

While every effort has been made to trace the owners of the
copyright material reproduced herein, the publishers
would like to apologise for any omissions and will be pleased
to incorporate missing acknowledgements
in future correspondence.

Text Copyright © 2009 Suzie Wilks and Deborah Gray

Illustrations by Allister Hardiman
Author photographs by Gilly Wheeler
Design & Images Copyright © 2009 Blue Angel Publishing
Edited by Tanya Graham and Annie Cruse

Chapter 2: "I have my standards. They may be low but I have them!" – Bette Midler
Chapter 8: "I don't believe in Astrology, I'm a Sagittarian and we are sceptical." – Arthur C. Clark
Chapter 11: A good place to meet a man is the drycleaners, these men usually
have jobs and bathe." – Rita Rudner

ISBN: 978-0-9805550-2-8
Library Cataloguing Number. 646.77
Subjects: Mate selection. Soul mates. Happiness. Love.

CONTENTS

A MESSAGE FROM THE AUTHORS

Welcome aboard!

You are about to embark on a life-changing journey towards love. Everyone is welcome to come along and all you need to bring with you is some honesty, optimism and your sense of humour.

If you have been looking for a loving and rewarding relationship but can't seem to find someone who is ready to go steady, we understand what you are going through.

If you've suffered heartbreak in the past, or been out with all the wrong people, we've made many of the same mistakes ourselves.

We are not claiming to be experts, but we do have a wealth of experience between us and this is what we would like to share with you to help you understand yourself, your relationships, and where you may have been going wrong in the past.

This book combines practical advice and emotional tips to help you take the relevant steps to finding a partner. This is not a self-help book in the typical sense but we do ask you to listen to yourself, define who you are and discover what you are really looking for.

So let this book be the first step on a new path. Use it to help you to find all the emotional essentials you need to take with you on your travels towards true happiness.

Before we begin on this journey, it's worth taking the time to explore: What does it mean to be emotionally available? It's one thing to be single and looking for a relationship, but being emotionally available is about being genuinely ready, in every sense, to embark on your next love-adventure. Before starting a new relationship, it's vitally important to ensure that you've truly moved on from any painful past experiences of love and learnt the lessons you needed to. You also need to learn to be your own true love and recognise exactly what it is that you bring to a partnership, before you can invite anyone else in to share the journey of your life with you. And that's where this book comes in. It's designed to navigate you through all the necessary steps along the way to finding you a mate.

Now, it's time to set sail to Destination Love.

CHECK-IN

Before you begin, it's important that you clear your life of infectious ideas and unwanted baggage. In this section we'll tell you about all the stuff you need to leave behind before you embark on this journey. Some people see nothing but the differences between the sexes, and never stop to think about the similarities – and yes, there are many.

Every individual is made up of life experiences. Each of us comes into a relationship with our own history, desires, wants, hopes and needs. It's unreasonable to say that all men are the same, just as it is ridiculous to say that all women are the same. The fact is, we are all human, and we all, ultimately, want the same things – to love and connect. Sure there are physical and emotional differences between the sexes, but just because men and women go about things in different ways doesn't necessarily mean that they come from different planets.

We all need to feel connected. We all need to give love and be loved. It is a basic human need, as necessary as food and water and air. But just because a person has the same body parts as you doesn't mean that they share the same ideals, hopes, fears or emotions.

There are plenty of emotional and demonstrative men out there, just as there are plenty of women who have difficulty communicating.

These traits are the result of our collected experience, not merely the characteristics of gender. So try to see people as people; the wonderful, different, colourful, individual human beings that we all are!

Sometimes we all need a reminder of the similarities that we share. Here are a few of them:

- We all want to feel appreciated. Nobody wants to feel their actions go unnoticed or feel that they are taken for granted.
- We want to feel desired by our partner.
- We want to feel admired by the one we are with.
- We would love to feel in a crowded room that we are the most special person to our partner in that room.

Keep these things in mind and you will find that your journey is not only a lot more pleasant, but a lot more interesting!

Wouldn't it be wonderful if we lived in a society where anger and disappointment made us irresistible?

14

COUNT YOUR BLESSINGS

Deb

Many people are fearful that they may never meet anyone or love again. This fear can affect you more than you may realise and can prevent potential partners from coming into your life. The energy around you radiates a despondency or negativity and can suggest that you are not emotionally available.

There is nothing more unattractive, unappealing or unsexy than people who are angry or disappointed with their lot in life. Some people can endure the most incredible heartbreak and devastation yet bounce back with a positive attitude and just get on with things. Others experience one small setback and become disillusioned and give up. Believe it or not, there is no great secret or magic formula to overcoming adversity. It's all a matter of forgiveness, acceptance and letting go.

There are some unkind people in the world – a fact that we all have to learn to live with. So how do you recover from someone doing you wrong? The biggest favour you can do yourself is to cut your losses and let it go. If you are consumed by anger you will not see opportunities that present themselves to you.

Envy is another infectious idea best left behind you. Don't waste time sitting around comparing yourself to others you believe to be more fortunate than you are. Surely you would be better channelling that energy into something productive and finding ways to improve the quality of your own life. You are losing out and letting yourself down when you compare yourself to others you consider to be luckier than you. There is nothing wrong with aspirations and working towards goals that you set yourself, you should take inspiration from people who are successful in life and love. But if you really must make comparisons, try comparing yourself to the few billion people who are less fortunate than you in the world – that might change your perspective.

If you are saddled with feelings of envy for someone else's partner, ask yourself if that person is worthy of such a destructive and consuming emotion. Analyse the qualities that person has that you think are appealing. If the reasons are materialistic and physical you still need to do a lot more work on yourself. If your envy is inspired by the fact they have great qualities, then you have some excellent standards to which you can aspire. Now you know there will be someone like that out there for you!

If you are in good health, have a roof over your head, and a job you enjoy, then you are already blessed in life. You are in a strong position to move forward and convert that negative energy into something positive. Try to feel passionate about feeling good. You will never find the person you are looking for if you are consumed by negative thoughts and emotions. It is time to count your blessings.

"When we spend a day in the company of regrets, we lose a day in the company of happiness."

Angry, envious or jaded people often forget one of life's most important rules - do not get upset over things you cannot change. Let's face it, there are plenty of positive changes we can make without sweating over the stuff we cannot change.

"I have my standards. They may
be low but I have them!"

EXCESS BAGGAGE

Suzie

If your mind is taken up with an ex-partner, you won't have the space for someone else to come in. It is very important that you leave such excess baggage behind you.

One of the biggest mistakes people make is hanging onto a partner from a past relationship, continually reinventing that person in their mind, and/or revisiting old memories time and again.

If this sounds like you, then take heart; there may be several reasons why you are doing this. Maybe because it's all you know; maybe because you need someone to think about when you feel lonely; maybe you haven't grieved for a lost love or let go of the pain of rejection; or maybe it's just nice to have someone to talk about as a single person in a world that sometimes seems made for couples.

Are you rewarding your ex with a Lifetime Achievement Award? You have already dedicated your past to them, don't let them take on a leading role in your future. LET THEM GO!

If you are pining for a lost love, ask yourself if you are remembering them as you wish they were, or how they really are. Are you holding on to a tiny bit of hope that they will one day come back? If so... LET IT GO!

If you felt a past relationship was wonderful but your partner left you because they didn't feel the same way, then it's time to face the truth. Sometimes love isn't reciprocated. Unrequited love is one of the greatest tragedies of humankind; without it we wouldn't have some of the most beautiful poetry or love songs ever written. Without it, you wouldn't know how to appreciate true love and kindness when it does come along or how to recognise a partner that truly values you. So... LET THEM GO!

Think over this past relationship. When you were involved in the relationship did you find yourself making excuses for your partner?

Have you ever said any of the following?
(You fill in the blanks.)

- 'He/she really is a nice person, it's just that ___'
- 'He/she would never do that ordinarily.
  It's because of ___!'
- 'Sorry he/she is late, it's just that ___!'
- 'I was hoping he/she would come too, but he/she is busy with___!

We all want to be involved with a loving, considerate and emotionally available partner who cares about us and who makes our relationship a priority. Was that what you actually had? Or is that what you imagine you had now that it's all over? You need to be entirely honest with yourself as you consider these questions. Were you truly valued in that relationship? If you think you were, then where is that person now?

So how do you let go of the past? Here's an exercise that might help.

LIST A	LIST B
Unreliable	Responsible
Unfaithful	Committed
Deceitful	Honest
Selfish	Considerate
Emotionally unavailable	Emotionally available
Disinterested	Caring
Erratic	Consistent
Pessimistic	Encouraging
Defensive	Open

Write out a résumé for your ex-partner. Be brutally honest about the facts but remember this is NOT a blame game, just a fact sheet to give you some perspective.

Above are some examples of words that may help you fill in your résumé. Add any others that are relevant to your situation.

When you have finished, look over your list and add up how many traits from each box your ex scored. If you notice a trend of words from List A then it should be quite apparent to you that your ex should remain exactly that - an ex!

If you see that your ex has an equal amount from both boxes then it's time to consider whether the negative traits outweigh the positive ones. For example, you may realise that no amount of caring, attentive and considerate actions can ever make up for cruelty or betrayal, whereas you might be inclined to overlook selfish behaviour if your partner is responsible, committed and honest. It's entirely up to you to decide what you need. Don't make any more excuses. Don't focus only on the positive traits of your ex when there were a plethora of negative ones too.

Be glad for what you had. Take the experiences of past loves, learn what you can, grow, and then... LET THEM GO.

It can take time to heal, so be gentle with yourself, but don't let your grief consume you any longer than it needs to. It will only hold you back from moving on, embracing life and meeting a new love.

It's time to focus on all the wonderful and exciting opportunities of love and romance that are waiting for you in the future!

Pack up the past and leave it well and truly behind you!

Learning to love yourself
is the secret to
a life-long relationship.

ALL ABOARD

Suzie

Well, you've checked in and, now that you're on board, before you get to know your fellow passengers, it's time for you to get to know and love yourself! In the following chapters we'll help you take a good look around at some prospective partners – and some types to avoid! But before you do, make sure, first and foremost, that YOU are someone you'd like to take this trip with.

Introduce Yourself

Before you can really get to know anyone else, it might be a good time to make sure that you know – and love – who YOU are.

"You can't love anyone until you love yourself."

You have probably heard these words many times before, so much so they have become clichéd. But have you ever really considered their meaning? Pretend for a moment that you have never heard those words before and think about what they actually mean, and why their meaning is essential for happiness and love.

It's quite simple. When things are going well in your life you feel like giving, sharing and loving. It could be something like a compliment, an award, or a promotion that lifts your spirits, or it could be something as simple as having a good hair day. When things are going well life seems a bit brighter, the weight lifts, you feel joyful and tolerant. Someone asks you to do something and without hesitation you say yes, happily and willingly.

The happiness that you enjoy in that moment extends to feelings of love towards yourself. You are more able and willing to give to others because you have more inner resources. You come home with a smile on your face and it stays there while you do the laundry, cook the dinner, pay the bills, take out the garbage... You feel fantastic, you're in a positive place and things don't seem to faze you. You are in the frame of mind where you are actually loving yourself and in this place, subconsciously, you also understand how someone else could love you too.

Now let's look at things through a different lens. You miss out on that promotion or award you felt you deserved, your hair looks flat and greasy and you feel unattractive, you put on last winter's jeans and you can't do up the button, nothing fits anymore, you fail an exam or miss your train. You feel down, agitated and annoyed. These feelings can quickly intensify and before you know it you are on a downward spiral into despondency. When someone asks you to do something for them, they may as well have asked you to climb Mt. Everest. You drag your feet and do it anyhow but without joy. You are often frustrated and can snap easily. You can't see the beauty in the world or in others, least of all in you. Instead of being kind to yourself at a time when you need the most nurturing, you take up unhealthy habits, let your personal grooming slide, or look for the answers at the bottom of a tub of ice cream. You can barely be bothered dragging yourself off the sofa. You don't really like being alone with yourself or feel like caring for yourself; you feel worthless.

There's not a lot of love here for anyone and that includes you. That's right, you! The you that you defend in arguments, the you that you want to put first, the you that cares more about what happens to you than anyone else. You have suddenly given up caring. Why would anybody else want to buy into that deal? The message you send to the world is, "Don't bother loving me, I have known me longest and the most intimately, and even I don't love me or treat me well. Obviously I am not worth it and I should know, I hang out with me all the time!"

"If you were selling your house, would you treat it like a dump and tell the world how ugly it is, let the garden overgrow and the maintenance slip, or would you treat it with love, care and attention pointing out its assets to potential buyers?"

Show the world that you are worthy of love. Give love to yourself as well as others and love is what you will get in return. If you often feel angry or lash out at those closest to you, if you are easily irritated about trivial things, if your tolerance of others is limited or you criticise others regularly, then your love for yourself is probably in need of some attention.

If you feel empty or worthless it's up to you to fill those painful spaces inside. It's up to you—and you alone—to fill yourself with love until you are overflowing. When you know for sure that you are okay on your own and you are full of love, you will begin to feel complete. You won't need anyone else to make you feel you are worthy of being loved. You'll know that if you care about yourself then somebody else will too. Love yourself with a whole heart, love yourself like you mean it! Only when you love yourself completely will you have the capacity to give love to another. And you will know how to do this, because you have been practising on you!

Easier said than done, you may be saying. Well, here's a fun exercise that is very powerful – and it works! You have to promise to start this today, and it is a commitment you need to stick to for the next few weeks.

First you need to choose a friend or relative that you feel close to and trust, perhaps someone who is also reading this book. Make a commitment to speak to that person or see that person as often as you can. At least once a week you need to commit to meeting face-to-face and the first day you meet is the day you start this exercise. Go and have a coffee together, a drink, or a bite to eat. During the time you spend together you are only to talk about yourselves. That is, you will each only talk about yourself every time you see or speak to one another for the next fourteen days.

Sound easy? Here's the challenging part.

Everything you say, and we mean everything that comes out of your mouth, must be a positive statement or praise! You are going to talk about how well you are doing at work, how beautiful/handsome you looked this morning when you left the house, how talented you are, how you just can't believe how amazing you are! You can talk about the past, the present and the future, and in every sentence you are going to gush – yes, gush! – about yourself. You are going to talk yourself up like you would a person you had just fallen in love with, the person of your dreams! This person that you admire so much, that you are getting to know and falling in love with is yourself. Remember the saying 'you never forget your first love'? Well - you are your first love! If you love yourself enough you will never forget how wonderful you are and how much you have to offer. You won't forget to value yourself as the remarkable, unique and special person you are – and neither will anyone else.

This might seem crazy at first but try it and stick to it. What have you got to lose? Besides, this exercise is a lot of fun. You will find yourself laughing at the things you come up with. Laughing is joy, joy is love. You may feel strange and silly at times, but let go of your inhibitions and enjoy it. You will notice how fantastic you feel and how wonderful life seems all of a sudden. How your posture improves and the spring has returned to your step. How you can't help but smile and radiate positive energy. Every day will feel great and you'll soon know why – you love someone who deserves everything you have to give and every bit of your unconditional love.

You're in love with you! Now that's really someone you can spend the rest of your life with!

This is not about vanity or egotism; this is a deep responsibility we have to ourselves and to others. Nurturing, loving and being grateful and thankful for who we are. It's not about me, me, me; it's about thank you, thank you, thank you, for me. It's about learning to love and be grateful, for being blessed and being the one and only wonderful you.

The problem with some people is they fall in love with anything - and then marry it!"

MENU

Deb

Now that you are feeling good about yourself, it's time to take a look around and see who's out there! Who are you looking for? Is it time to look for a different type of person?

Do you look for the right ingredients in a relationship or do you settle for just anything? You may have high standards in other areas of your life but you let them slip when it comes to finding love. You wouldn't attempt to create a gourmet meal out of mouldy old food, so why wouldn't you look for the best ingredients when it comes to creating a happy and enduring relationship? You need a formula for success, not a recipe for disaster.

If you are feeling anxious and scared about being alone and believe you will be lucky if you find 'anyone', chances are you will probably settle for second best. When you feel this way you give out the wrong signals to the universe – you want a partner and anyone who is vaguely acceptable will do. A hungry shopper is a bad shopper. Everything on the shelf is tempting when you haven't eaten in a while! So take time to pause and think objectively. Do you really want just anyone? Are you prepared to set up the most important person in the world – you – with any old person who comes along? Are you prepared to fill your shopping trolley with junk food to satisfy short-term cravings?

Don't spend all that time and effort learning to love yourself only to sell yourself short in the end. You are only going to create more disappointment and dismay in your life. And that will put you right back where you started.

It's time to write a shopping list for the discerning shopper that you are! Write down everything you want in a partner, whether it's superficial or extremely deep and meaningful. Reflect on this list, and keep it in mind when you are out and about. Of course it's unlikely that you will meet someone who fills every criterion (although it's not entirely impossible!) so you must decide which traits are mandatory. If you are a vegan perhaps a carnivore is not the answer for you. If you love to talk, then the strong silent type won't be much use. No matter how many other qualities your partner may have that seem appealing to you, eventually the one that irritates you most will be all you can see when the honeymoon period is over. And don't go thinking they will change for you. Yes, people can change, but you should never enter a relationship thinking everything will be perfect when 'he stops doing this' or 'she starts doing that'. Believing that your life will begin at some point in the future is a mistake. Your life has already begun; you are living it right now.

Write your list carefully, decide what is important and what you are prepared to be flexible on. Keep an open mind, be objective and, above all, maintain a sense of humour. Also, be open to the idea that someone may come along who is completely different to what you had in mind, someone who doesn't meet many of your criteria, someone who breaks the mould of every person you have been with in the past. If the attraction is there, then why not try something different? Don't just settle for whatever comes your way, but if the spark is there, it could be worth exploring.

Remember, you don't need to settle for leftovers. It's a rich feast out there, and healthy, tasty food is in plentiful supply.

If he hasn't called you in a couple of weeks
and you have no idea why, chances are he is not
lost in the Amazon crying out your name.

FANTASY ISLAND

Deb

Have you ever fantasised about meeting a gorgeous lover on a deserted island who only had eyes for you, or watched a movie and imagined that you were the one being swept up in the arms of the leading man? Or even that someone you met through work or saw on the train walks up and announces that you are the person they've been looking for their whole life?

It's a rare person who hasn't indulged in a fantasy every once in a while. Fantasyland is a great escape from the day-to-day grind. Fantasy keeps us sane when the workload is heavy or the day is long and boring. Fantasy is particularly exhilarating when we've been single for a long time. Everything and anything happens on Fantasy Island where no one but you is running the show. You decide what happens and who it happens with. It's like watching the perfect movie inside your own head!

However, thinking about Fantasy Island can consume you. It is important to keep the real world in constant view.

Perhaps a quick reality check might be in order. Ask yourself:

- When was the last time a stranger knocked on your door and you fell in love?

- When did that ex, who was extremely happy in another relationship, ever return to you?

- Do you take, 'I like you as a friend,' to mean something more?

- If someone buys you a drink do you presume a romantic intention?

- Do you think anyone of the opposite sex who says hello and smiles fancies you?

If you have answered yes to any of these questions, you may have overstayed your welcome in the land of daydreams.

Sure, any of the above possibilities have worked out for someone somewhere, but if you spend too long on Fantasy Island, chances are you will misinterpret nearly everything anyone of the opposite sex says to you.

Look at and think about what the person of interest in your life does, not what they say. You will soon know if someone is attracted to you by their actions. If they ask you on a date, or you ask them on a date and they say yes, or at any available opportunity they talk to you or do kind deeds for you, then you have a good indication of their intentions. If someone is interested in you they will try to let you know. That's what you would do, right?

We have all seen soaps like 'The Bold and the Beautiful' and it's fun to fantasise about living in a world that is totally unreal: no bills, no garbage to take out, no washing up or ironing, no boring job, everyone looking perfect all the time with an endless supply of money and fabulous floral arrangements – as far from the real world as you can possibly get!

It's a certainty that some people are only attracted to slender blondes or buxom brunettes, or toned and tanned athletes, or witty intellectuals. Some older men and women may need younger 'trophy' partners to validate themselves. We can't change people's preferences or choices; we just have to learn to live with it when someone we like doesn't like us back. However, what you can do is have a good understanding of the type of person you are attracted to so that you can identify them if your paths cross. Meeting potential dates or new people requires effort on your part. It's not always easy finding emotionally available, interesting partners, but no amount of fantasising is going to be enough to deliver them to your door.

It is wonderful to dream and have a wish list of your perfect mate – Brad Pitt, Elle McPherson – you get the picture. Some people are still living a teenage dream of the perfect person with the perfect everything that will make everything just perfect! This is unrealistic. People are colourful, unique and different, and no one – not even fabulous you – is perfect!

So let's have a good look at one fantasy we all have. Ourselves. When you look in the mirror do you see ALL of you? Are you honest with yourself and others about what you want and what you have to offer?

Would you date you?

Here's an exercise that will help you decide whether you've strayed onto Fantasy Island:

1. Sit down and write out honestly what you have to offer as a person and your relationship strengths and weaknesses. Remember to be totally HONEST. This list is for your eyes only.

2. Now, write down what you are looking for in a mate.

3. "Marry" them together.

How does it look? Are your expectations in a potential mate compatible with your list about yourself? This is the beginning of what a relationship is all about - looking honestly at a potential partner and looking honestly at YOURSELF!

If your two lists are very different, it's time to step out of the clouds and back into reality!

UTOPIA

Deb

Welcome to the land of Utopia, a place where everything is oh-so-rosy and everyone you meet is seductive and alluring. Utopia is not far from Fantasy Island and is the place many people go when a marriage or a relationship has hit troubled waters.

A stay on Utopia is a miracle cure, a heavenly experience, a place you can visit to cheat on your partner or with someone else's and not feel guilty about it. No matter what role you are playing, it's all pretty damn good until the novelty wears off. Utopia on a good day means a heavenly, blissful experience; on a bad day, when the weather changes without warning, it turns into a very rough experience.

When you get involved in an affair on Utopia, your partner hangs onto every word you say, laughs at all your jokes, listens to your problems intently, and is compassionate and caring. You feel alive and attractive and your lover can't wait to jump into bed with you because you are so desirable. It's easy to push aside the fact that you or your lover is married or in a steady relationship.

When you are on Utopia there are no problems to share, no chores to do, no mortgage to pay and no children to look after. Stolen moments are so seductive and the sex is amazing. You both take great care over your appearance before each meeting and always make a point of seeing each other when you are looking and feeling your very best. Meanwhile your real life partner remains back in the real world.

On Utopia every day is filled with fantasy and delicious, stolen moments. You are oblivious to the fact that you are participating in destroying your lover's relationship. You tell yourself that your lover's partner doesn't understand them or no longer has time for the marriage. You conveniently forget that your new lover has not made time for their real-life partner because they are spending all their free time on Utopia with you.

You feel alive and have a glow that reminds you of the early stages of past relationships; the only difference is you have forgotten that nothing is real on Utopia. You cannot judge your new lover objectively when you have come together in a relationship of deceit and duplicity.

The only time you may get a better insight into your lover's true personality is when either of you decide to leave Utopia unexpectedly. Your lover may suddenly develop regrets or may realise that if they invested the same amount of time and effort into their 'real' relationship they might be able to recapture the passion they once shared.

Or you may start to wonder if your lover was single and available whether you would want to be with someone who is happy to cheat. Maybe you would prefer someone with stronger principles and more integrity.

All too often you will come to realise you have been wasting time in a fool's paradise and your lover's real-life partner has been living in a loveless relationship. Or you will feel terrible as it slowly becomes apparent this was just an escape from reality, and that you are the cause of so much unhappiness for someone else.

Married people, men or women, rarely leave their partner for the person they are having an affair with. Often the affair is just a brief escape from some turbulence in the marriage. If a married man tells you he will 'one day' leave his wife for you he is usually lying. If he really wanted to be in an honest, committed and respectful relationship with you he would have left his wife already. You are a fool to believe otherwise, no matter what he tells you.

Don't waste time on Utopia. Don't kid yourself that things are different in your particular situation; they are not. It's all the same: lies, deceit and, ultimately, pain. If you feel you really are in love with someone who is attached, wait until they are single before you hook up. That way you can hold your head up proudly and enjoy the honest, open and rewarding relationship that you deserve.

HORROR SCOPES

Deb

Are you ruled by the Zodiac?

Will you only date particular star signs? If so, perhaps it's time to get your head out of the stars and come back to Earth.

Too many single people pin all their faith and hopes on their weekly horoscope, desperately clinging to any positive sign, despondent and dejected if their prospective new partner's planets are not aligned with theirs.

What signs are you compatible with? Who is your love sign? Sadly these questions – and the resulting wrong answers – rule too many people's lives. Do you really believe millions of people all over the planet share the same fate as you this week simply because they share the same sign? A starving child in Ethiopia, a soldier in Iraq, a Massai warrior in Africa, Oprah Winfrey, Prince Charles, Charles Manson?

If you are like most people who are looking for meaning, you may have spent considerable time and money seeking answers from numerology, tarot cards, psychics, horoscopes and so on. Life is not perfect and many of us have had more than enough difficulty dealing with past and present misadventures to contemplate what may lie ahead. So it is no surprise that we look to others for guidance, especially when they claim to have all the right answers and somehow know what we want to hear. But how can you expect to find all of life's answers in under 50 words in your daily star sign column or in a thirty-minute session from a tarot card reader?

There are some talented and genuine psychics around and there is definitely something mystical about the sun, moon and stars. But while it is certainly uplifting and inspiring to contemplate life in this way, we must remember our reality is here and now on Earth and it is unwise to let any mystical philosophy completely take over our lives, no matter how convincing it may seem. There is no denying that some people share an uncanny similarity to the typical characteristics of their star sign and it can be an interesting subject to explore. Just don't let it blind you to reality!

We have all been guilty at one time or another of reading too much into predictions, desperately seeking hope where there is none. How many times have you read your ex's stars praying for a sign they still care? Spending too much time grieving over a lost love is futile, and if you stop and think for a minute and are completely honest with yourself, you might pray that the stars don't deliver them back to you!

Starting a new relationship or finding the perfect partner requires effort. Just because a psychic tells you that your soul mate is about to come into your life doesn't mean you just sit back and wait, only to discover later you have wasted precious time and become complacent living under the false hope of a prediction.

You will not find love just by reading the stars or pursuing other mystical lifelines; you need to actively look for it. Whether that is by joining a sporting group, socialising at singles' events, keeping your eyes peeled at the supermarket, or asking friends to introduce you to single people they know — these are the things that will lead you in the right direction towards meeting the person of your dreams. Be realistic, be proactive, and most of all, keep your feet on the ground.

Only when you find the one you've been looking for and have based your relationship in reality will you have real stars in your eyes! That's when the true magic begins! That's when the planets are truly aligned!

FROTH AND BUBBLE

Deb

It's wonderful to daydream about your fabulous destination, but don't forget to have a good time along the way. Here are a few on-board activities that will make your journey all the more memorable.

Fabulous Flirting

Remember when it was safe to talk to strangers? Remember the days when you could give someone at work a compliment and did not fear accusations of sexual harassment?

Whatever happened to fabulous flirting? If you have just left a long-term relationship, or have not dated for a while, chances are you have not practised flirting for some time. Try to think back to the last time you flirted. Remember how enjoyable it felt?

Flirting is giving a thoughtful compliment, flirting is playful and fun, and flirting should boost your self-esteem. Have you ever noticed when you are in a flirtatious mood everything seems to go your way? That is because people are responding to how you are treating them and are receptive to your friendly, flirtatious behaviour. Your personality is radiant and people are reacting to it.

Flirting is not necessarily sexual. Jokes and humour are great ways to flirt. When you flirt with people, they know you are genuinely interested, which helps them warm to you.

Flirting is an art; the more you do it the better you'll be at it! But it should not be misdirected. You should never use flirting as an excuse for making lewd or crude comments about someone. It is definitely not about dodgy pick-up lines (You know what would look great on you? Me). We've heard them all before and no one wants to know. Dirty jokes are an immediate turn off for some people and if you are crude or risqué while flirting, you may end up embarrassed or worse. Best to save that for when you know the person much better.

It is also not a licence for women to go around feeling a man's body whenever the mood strikes. (Why do some women think they can walk up to a guy in a bar and feel free to pinch him on the bum, or feel his muscles? Those same girls would be mortified if a guy were to do that to them uninvited!)

In fact there is no need to be too outrageous – less is definitely more. In the initial phase of flirting play it safe; respect is the key. Flirting is not always a precursor to sex, and when used genuinely it can be fun for everyone. People should respond positively if you flirt with style.

These tips will help:

- **Remember to feel confident when you flirt. If you are not being sleazy you have no reason to panic.**

- **Don't get too close too soon. Most people feel uncomfortable when a new acquaintance stands too close.**

- Body language is important. Good posture communicates self-confidence.

- Your voice is an important flirting tool. To some people a voice can be very seductive. Speak clearly and loud enough to be heard, but avoid shouting.

- Eye contact is a very powerful flirting tool but it is important to focus on the person's face. Don't let your eyes wander over their body as this can make some people feel uncomfortable. If the person you are flirting with is shy, penetrating eye contact can be too familiar too soon.

- Flirting feedback is important and you have to pay attention to the signals to see if there is a genuine level of interest or if you are facing a subtle rejection.

Don't let a fear of rejection hold you back from flirting and don't think for a minute that others will perceive you as desperate. Take a compliment at face value, enjoy the experience and do not think too deeply about the reason behind it.

Flirting should become a daily ritual for everybody!

"I met my wife at the door and she was only wearing a g-string. Unfortunately she was just arriving home."

EN ROUTE

Deb

Feeling Frisky

If you have been single for a while, you probably crave to feel the loving arms of another person around you. This strong need for affection is part of being human. It is during these times of physical desire that you are most likely to jump into bed with just about anyone and this is where the trouble can begin.

Some people are quite content to indulge in casual sex, often when they are going through a challenging time, still recovering from a lost relationship, or just not interested in getting involved. Casual sex can be very convenient, but it can also be a minefield of pain and misunderstanding.

It is time to look at your history. You may need to remind yourself that you participated in creating each sexual experience and so you must also take responsibility. Remember it takes two to do the tango and you chose to be part of the dance! If you believe your history indicates you are guilty of some poor judgement, and you feel you lose perspective and get too emotionally involved too soon, perhaps it might be wise to 'shut up shop' before deciding if the person you fancy is the one for you. Controlling your sexual desire is not always easy, especially if you are deeply attracted to someone and feeling frisky, but you must remind yourself your heart is precious, you are special, and if you are falling for someone you need to investigate what is going on above their shoulders and find out if they feel the same way as you.

The true definition of casual sex is a one-night stand. Anything further than that and you have developed a relationship of sorts. Often these casual relationships are 'booty calls' – convenient situations where you can call up your partner, get it on, then go home again without any further involvement in each other's lives. This is fine if that's what you are into. But you're probably not! Chances are you are looking for more meaning and commitment - because you are reading this book!

Don't make the mistake of thinking that a casual encounter will ultimately lead to a fulfilling relationship. While this may happen in some instances, it is rare. Continuing to see someone on a casual basis as a bunk-bunny, hoping that one day they will grow to love you, can sometimes lead to disappointment. Remember, some people will tell you anything you want to hear if it means they can ultimately get what they want.

If you have a history of casual encounters, or have always had a few sexual buddies 'on the side', ask yourself if this has prevented you from meeting the perfect mate. Most people who have regular casual sex miss genuine opportunities by becoming complacent and comfortable in relationships of convenience that never evolve beyond the physical. If this sounds familiar then you need to think about why you have behaved in this way. If it was just because you didn't want to get involved or were too busy, then that's fair enough. But if it was out of some deeper fear of commitment or of getting hurt then it's probably a good idea for you to seek some guidance in order to help yourself heal.

The exercises in this book are the first steps towards learning to love and value yourself. If you believe you have some deep-seated, emotional problems then we recommend you seek professional advice. Find a qualified counsellor you can trust if you have suffered childhood abuse or any severe trauma throughout your life. This will be an invaluable step towards freeing yourself from the pain and fear that may be holding you back.

If you were to write a few pages about your sexual experiences would they follow a similar pattern? Would you describe yourself as affectionate, romantic or aloof? If you are possessive or jealous, how have you handled a one-night stand? What are you seduced by? When and why do you have casual sex? Are you unfulfilled with only one partner and need casual sex to keep you on an emotional high? Do you prefer tempestuous casual relationships where you deliberately create conflict with a partner and use it to create excitement? Or maybe you just enjoy the thrill of the chase? Take a good look at your sexual history – what you are happy with or perhaps disappointed about, review it honestly and then decide how you want to manage your sex life in the future.

"A good place to meet a man is at the drycleaners, these men usually have jobs and bathe."

DATE, DATE, DATE

Okay, so you are now in a new and exciting phase in your life. You love yourself, value yourself, you know what you have to offer and what you are looking for in a partner, and you're feeling confident and excited about your life. You're happy and proud about who you are, inside and out, and you know that some very lucky person is going to have the chance to share some of that.

Yes it's time to date, date, date! Here are a couple of things you need to do that you may not have done in the past. Firstly, say YES to as many dates as you can! If and when you are invited out, think 'yes' first. Be open to new experiences and to people.

Follow your instincts though – if somebody comes across as a 'Casanova-type' or is inappropriate, or your gut feeling tells you to keep away from a person, then say no. When you meet a prospective partner what you FEEL when you are around that person is what you should listen to. This is your intuition speaking to you, and no credentials, books or experts (no matter how close they come) will necessarily give you the feeling that says inside you, "I want to spend time with this person. I want to be around this person. I would like to see this person again."

Let's take a moment to review your expectations. Think about which list best describes your date's desired characteristics:

LIST A	LIST B
Handsome / beautiful	Honest
Wealthy	Sincere/warm
Successful	Independent
Tall	Attractive
Fit/Slim	Confident/talented
Large pecs/big breasts	Funny
Charming	Emotionally mature
Cool/fashionable	Open

Many people choose from list A and then complain about being alone or unfulfilled. Discard your unrealistic expectations and fantasies and replace them with a genuine list of the real traits that will fulfil you. Keep it fair and realistic; make a list that is obtainable and honest and not just a fantasy.

If you are the type of person who likes doing the asking you should take the plunge and ask someone out. Dating different people is great for two reasons.

• You will only recognise the 'right one' when you find them, and that might take a few - or many - different dates.

- Dating different people will help you down the track when you're in a loving and fulfilling relationship. You will understand and appreciate how unique and special your partner is and not take them for granted, or think there are hundreds just like them!

We don't truly know the value of someone until we fully understand that there is no one else like them. Remember also that there is nobody else in this entire world exactly like you. You are unique and special. There is only one you, so go on these dates with confidence knowing that you are special and you deserve the best life has to offer.

Remember to be available and receptive to new experiences. You may be walking your dog, picking up your dry cleaning or going to a party when out of the blue a moment will arise. People often say they met their partner when they least expected it.

So step outside and start participating, you're not going to find a partner while you are sitting at home. We know you may not feel like going out alone again, but it's different now. How exciting! You are ready for new adventures and there is possibility everywhere you go! Look around, see and be receptive to emotionally available potential partners that in the past you would not have been able to identify at first glance! Your new-found confidence, feelings of self-love and dating lessons will give you the tools to project that you are available and receptive.

From now on when you meet people, don't worry about assumptions – assuming he or she is taken or think it's too forward to ask a stranger out. Just ask! The answer may not always be the one you want to hear but at least you will have an answer.

"I was on a date with this really hot model. Well, it wasn't really a date date. We just ate dinner and saw a movie. Then the plane landed." – Dave Attell

When you go on a date make sure your outlook is positive and open. Get excited and look forward to it. Don't go out with pre-conceived ideas or expectations. You must always remain open to the experience and try not to make judgements before you give someone a chance.

A date is not a time to let out all your emotional frustrations and bitter and painful thoughts. A date is not a counselling session. If you are still hung up on your ex or have one stalking you, sort it out first before you start to date. Go back to the beginning of this book and make sure that you are truly ready and emotionally available.

Whether you were the one who did the asking out or, have been asked out, it is both parties' responsibility to try to make it an enjoyable occasion. Make the other person feel important by making an effort to dress appropriately. Respect each other's time, be punctual, polite and listen attentively to your date. Ask questions, but be mindful it is the first date and you don't need to know everything right here, right now. It is important to ask appropriate personal questions, but too many personal questions on a first date can be frightening to some people. Be honest about you, talk from the heart and be real, knowing who you are and liking yourself for those qualities. Be yourself. This is about finding a suitable partner to have a long-term relationship with. Begin with openness and integrity. Be real.

Enjoy yourself even if you can't see a date turning into love. Make the most of the experience, practice your skills, and be happy being there. You are on a date; they are supposed to be fun! Even if this person is not 'the one', they could become a good friend and who knows? They might even introduce you to the future love of your life.

BURIED TREASURE

Deb

Dating at any age should be fun, but let's face it, as we mature most of us can't help feeling a little sceptical and cynical about the subject. And for good reason, many of us have worries or doubts as we enter the dating arena. For some even the word 'dating' might fill you with dread or panic attacks.

If you are feeling distressed by the mere mention of the subject then make yourself a cup of tea or pour a glass of wine, brace yourself, sit down and calmly read on.

You probably haven't revealed all your grown up dating misfortunes, even to your closest friends, so we're going to fast-track your healing process. But before we do, let's share a couple of familiar scenarios that may remind you that you are not alone.

Dinner Parties

In this scene, some well-meaning friends have invited you to a dinner party to make up the numbers. The talk mainly centres on married things and though you try to fit in, you start to feel as though you really don't belong. You know a couple of the guests are insecure and you become acutely aware not to linger too long when talking with their partners; you have no desire to offend anyone but start to feel that innocent conversing is being misconstrued as flirtatious or seductive behaviour. You try not to talk to anyone for too long, thank your hosts and are glad when you are finally home again where you can relax.

Bars

Feeling like you are running out of options, you try out some new inner-city bars, where you quickly come to realise that times have changed since you were last on the singles scene and you can barely understand the lingo. A quick glance around the room reveals that you are surrounded by young men with fit bodies and gorgeous young women wearing skimpy outfits. You cannot help but notice that you are standing out in the crowd for all the wrong reasons. No wonder you feel uncomfortable. Suddenly you spot someone heading your way and smiling, and for a moment you think that maybe you've got what it takes after all. Excitedly, and with a flourish they introduce themselves as either: a) a good friend of one of your children or, b) they recognise you as a business associate of one of their parents. It is right about now that you order a double martini.

Over 35 nights

Over 35 singles' nights can often mean over 55, with men in some circles calling these events 'grab a granny night'. The women are often perceived as a 'sure thing' and arrive with their clothes clinging in all the wrong places and revealing far too much cleavage. The men are usually wearing too much jewellery and/or cologne and are often sporting a comb-over. You try not to be judgemental but you know that this is definitely not the place for you. You slip out quietly, desperate to get home and curl up in bed with a favourite book.

Blind Dates

Friends set you up with on a date, based entirely on the fact that you are single. They are convinced they have found your soul mate and they've made you excited too – this person sounds perfect! You soon discover that single is the only thing you have in common and your dear friends seem to have completely overlooked the fact that your companion has been recently released from jail, is gay, a player, or recently bereaved.

Internet Dating

Internet dating is often successful, but not knowing whether someone is being entirely honest about their age, situation or looks can prove disastrous. Sure, you should not always be judged by your age, height, weight and appearance, but there's a lot to be said for physical attraction. You may get along really well while online, and you believe that they are being honest when they say that, yes, the photo they sent you really was taken last week when they were down at the marina with their yacht, but how can you ever really be sure? How do you know whether anything they say or show you is real? You probably told a few white lies yourself!! Knowing only too well age is paramount on the web of love you panic at 40 and knock off 5 years on your personal profile and send a flattering photo taken when you were 30. If you do decide to meet up, you may be pleasantly surprised. Or you may be so alarmed by what you see that you pack your bags and jump on the next plane to Timbuktu.

Okay, so does any of that sound vaguely familiar? If not, then you are either doing better than most or you don't get out enough. Most of us have had a few strange experiences with mature dating, and this is often compounded by the fact that we feel more vulnerable than younger people. Despite all this, try to keep in mind that you don't need to protect yourself with emotional armour to enter the dating arena. You just need to be aware and have a bit of courage.

If someone has been unkind or insensitive to you on a past date take comfort in knowing that everyone – every single person in the world – will grow older eventually (if they are lucky) and if they find themselves single they will soon start to identify with exactly how you are feeling at this point in time. Trust us, you are not alone.

Times have changed, we are living longer, looking and acting younger, and divorce is much more common. However, modern society no longer has a sense of community life, people lead more solitary lives, living for work and dwelling in lonely apartment blocks. If you want to meet people, you are going to have to be more proactive.

Mature dating is not for the faint-hearted, and confidence and self-love are crucial to your success. But let's look at the positives; we may not be able to turn back the clock but we also have some sure-fire secret weapons. Our wealth of experience has blessed us with a great understanding of the realities of life. As older people we have survived divorce, loss, menopause, periods, erection problems, depression, bitterness, rotten jobs, financial ruin – things that many younger people have yet to experience. We have lived to tell the tale! And what a wonderful, interesting companion that makes you! Every experience you've had, whether positive or negative, has added to what you have to offer a potential partner. You are a person who has pretty much seen everything and is more tolerant, forgiving and compassionate for it.

So take a good look in the mirror; admire your maturing features, welcome the fact that your body has changed; eat well, get lots of exercise and plenty of rest. Smile. Dress to suit your body type and your age, no matter what your preference in clothes and style. Look back at all your life experiences and uncover your buried treasure! If you are in a rut, make a conscious effort to get out of it: volunteer to do some charity work, change jobs, take up a new hobby. Be glad that your people skills have improved over the years, that you have a better understanding of who you are, and although you may not know where you are going, you certainly know where you have been.

ABLUTIONS

'Ablutions' refers to a collection of habitual activities designed to bring about physical cleanliness and personal hygiene.

You are pretty much emotionally on track and just about ready for a relationship; your self-esteem is good and you are feeling positive, flirtatious and receptive to potential partners, who should hopefully be responding to the new you – unless you are fraught with bad habits. The advice in this chapter might seem obvious to most people, but just in case you've forgotten...

If anything is likely to scare away a potential partner it's a bad habit. But the question is - are they are actually bad habits or simply conflicting tastes? What may be extremely irritating to one person may go unnoticed by another, but if you think your behaviour is the likely problem when it comes to getting people to spend more time with you, then you need to look at ways to curb your social indiscretions.

Here are a few tips that hopefully should be obvious to you - but if they're not, take heed!

Table-top Trauma

Table manners vary dramatically in different parts of the world and while some people will not give them a second thought, others will be unforgiving in their judgement of what they consider to be socially acceptable table etiquette. Dinner will be an important event early in your new relationship, so demolishing your meal in record time can ruin the ambiance of the evening. Some cultures prefer to eat with their hands, and while knives and forks were once only available to the aristocracy, modern society is blessed with the opportunity to eat in a civilised manner - so make sure you use them correctly! A knife and fork handled incorrectly can be very unattractive. Don't wield them around like dangerous weapons – it's not very conducive to a relaxing meal! Talking with your mouth full is also an enormous turn-off, so swallow before you speak. It's also a good idea to abstain from licking the plate or sucking on a juicy bone. These things are best kept to times when you are dining in solitude.

Bodily Functions

Cover your mouth when you cough and sneeze and use tissues rather than a handkerchief. With cold and flu viruses rampant in society, it's far more hygienic to throw your bugs in the bin rather than carry them around in your pocket or up your sleeve.

It is very difficult to get excited about bad breath. Regular teeth cleaning at the dentist, gum check ups and a good dose of mouthwash will help.

Grooming is a matter of personal preference but remember it also impacts on your self-confidence. There is no doubt that if you look good, you feel good. Dirty hair, nails and clothes do not send off a positive vibe to others that you care or respect yourself.

The Boozer's Blues

Unfortunately, most single people only think of looking for a potential partner in a bar, but if you're not much of a drinker then chances are you are not going to enjoy watching people unravel or become untidy as the night progresses. If you have ever found yourself a little tipsy you may recall boring a potential love interest with a deep and meaningless conversation, divulging all the details of your personal or professional life, unaware that their eyes are glazing over as they look around the room for an escape route. Yet, strangely, you still find yourself truly fascinating! Such is the power of alcohol! The following morning often sheds a totally different light on things and you cringe as you slowly recall the events of the previous evening.

Alcohol is a great social lubricant and in moderation can be very seductive and enjoyable, just try not to view it as "a cup of courage". It is also important to be mindful that some people hold a very different view of it and other people's religious beliefs forbid it. So if you enjoy indulging in a cocktail or two it might be wise to consider dating someone who is not a teetotaller.

Smokin' Joe

Many people absolutely refuse to go out with anyone who smokes tobacco and in today's society it can sometimes seem like an illegal drug with smokers forced to get their fix outside in the freezing cold. Cigars are also a matter of personal choice. For some people the smell of a cigar or cigarette is an aphrodisiac while others are revolted by just the mere thought of it. To a non-smoker, a smoker stinks beyond belief. Would you stick your tongue in an ashtray? If you smoke and you are spending time in the company of a non-smoker, try to go without for a while or at least get some decent breath mints and wash your hands after smoking. Better still, try to quit! Your body will love you for it.

"I've quit smoking. I feel better, I smell better, and it's safer to drink out of old beer cans around the house." - Roseanne

Eau de B.O.

Body odour is a big turn off. We all get sweaty and smelly at times, and sometimes deodorant can fail us, especially if suffering from a hormonal imbalance, or if we are overcome with nerves or just from wearing synthetic fabrics. But you can usually control when you meet your new partner, so have a shower before you get together and this will definitely give you the edge. If B.O. is a problem for you, don't meet directly after a hard day's work in the sun or straight after a workout at the gym. And remember that strong foods such as garlic come out in the pores of the skin so consider what you eat on the day leading up to your big date. Before you go out, freshen up and show your new friend the respect they deserve.

Listen up!

Great self-confidence, impeccable grooming and perfect manners are all very desirable qualities but it is also important to consider another highly sought after trait in a partner – the ability to be a good listener. There is nothing more disappointing than when you are deep in conversation with someone and you suddenly realise they are not listening. This is often because they are more interested in what they are about to say next. There is an art to conversation; it is vital to ask questions and then listen to the answers. Everyone's taste is different, and you might prefer the quiet and mysterious type or the outgoing extrovert, but it is still important that you care enough to listen to what they have to say.

Take time to consider these pointers and, although they may seem incredibly obvious to some, others may not have thought about them at all. It could very well be the reason why things aren't going so well for you when you are meeting new people. So step back and look at yourself through the eyes of others and be aware of the differences in taste and personal preference. If you try to be the best person you can be and take pride in your presentation and appearance you'll have no end of people eager to spend time in your company!

74

PASSPORT TO LOVE

Deb

Think back to when you were young and innocent and had very few expectations about loving and dating. Remember when life was far less complicated and there were no real pressures in your day to day life? You might even have a smile on your face now thinking back to how inexperienced you were in all areas of life, how blissfully ignorant!

Try our approach to recapture some of that young spirit in you and to once again embrace that openness and lack of fear.

Step 1: *Lighten Up*

Let's rewind you back to a place where you feel free of emotional baggage. Before you leave home to catch up with friends or go on a date, try this simple affirmation exercise. It may help, especially if you need to let go of any stress or negative energy in your life.

Calm yourself.

Lie down on the floor or on a bed lying on your back. Close your eyes and breathe very deeply and slowly, in through the nose and out through the mouth. Tell yourself you are going to let go of all your troubles and think only lovely, calming thoughts. Think about how wonderful you are. Can you feel your body relaxing? If you still feel tense, keep breathing slowly and telling yourself that all your troubles will disappear just for today. Imagine them slowly leaving your body. As you feel them disappear, tell yourself that you can worry about them another day. Keep breathing and reaffirm that today you have no problems; today all you feel is peace and love. Relax your body and feel the tension slowly slip away.

Now say to yourself this quote from Michael Leunig's "The Prayer Tree".

"Let it out; let it go, let it all unravel. Let it free, and it can be a path on which to travel."

If you are feeling really stressed, it might be worth buying a relaxation tape or listening to some gentle music as well.

Step 2: *Think Positive*

Talk to yourself and explain how you are going out to meet new people or are going on a date and you are only going to feel free and happy. Remind yourself that you also deserve to give yourself the night off from problems, that you are emotionally available and you want to meet people that are fun. There is no pressure or expectation. Try to spend fifteen minutes relaxing your body and your mind so that when you go out you have stripped away the layers of emotional armour that have become your protection over the years.

Before you leave the house, look in the mirror one last time, you should look a little more relaxed and you should certainly feel it. Remind yourself one more time: tonight you are forgetting all problems or pain, because tonight you want to have fun and you want to be aware of the same positive energy in others. You will feel light and bright, and for good reason, because tonight you are totally carefree. When you are free of emotional baggage you will no longer feel the heavy burden that weighed you down and felt like boulders on your shoulders. And other people will sense this when they meet you.

Are you trying to be discovered...
or afraid you will be?

EMOTIONAL INTELLIGENCE

One of the most important items you should have plenty of for your travels is emotional intelligence. This will take you further and guide you better than all the travel brochures and books combined.

So what exactly is emotional intelligence? Psychologists have spent many years studying this complex theory but we're going to keep it simple: emotional intelligence is the ability to integrate thinking and feeling to make optimal decisions. If you have a high emotional intelligence you would:

- Have a clear understanding of who you are.
- Be able to understand and manage yourself and your emotions; be able to self-reflect.
- Think outside your own reality and have empathy and compassion for others.
- Be able to work through difficult issues in relationships.
- Communicate your feelings honestly and openly.

- Be able to listen, comprehend and absorb another person's words.

- Be intuitively aware of another person's emotional needs.

Most people continue to make the same mistakes with emotions and relationships, recovering from a previous hurt only to jump back in and do the same thing all over again, each time with a different person. In order to have satisfying and successful relationships, we must learn to become emotionally intelligent.

So how do you learn emotional intelligence?

From an early age we are taught how to achieve. We are encouraged to do well at school so we can go on to become successful in life. As adults we spend most of our time earning money to support the family, pay the bills and put food on the table. The importance of hard work is instilled in us from an early age – everyone respects a hard worker. We sometimes hide behind layers of protection - career, money, awards - as a way to avoid facing our true selves and those who love us.

Many people invest a great deal of time and money in their education, and it is certainly a worthwhile investment to make. But how often do you hear someone talk about how much they have invested in their emotional intelligence? Probably never. It's hard to imagine someone chatting to you at a party telling you about how much time they've spent developing their listening skills recently. Or how they've really learnt to open up and connect to their partner on a whole new level. When we meet new people in a social situation, one of the first questions out there is, 'What do you do for a living?' Yes, it's an interesting conversation starter, but we are allowing ourselves to be defined by what we do rather than who we are. People form an opinion of us simply by hearing about our occupation.

Now ask yourself, does your job fully describe you? Is that all you are? Is that all you have to offer as a rich, colourful, living, breathing human being with a heart and soul? What about the rest of you, the layers of you that people don't see? Interestingly, it is these qualities – the human ones – that are lovable and desirable, not the fact that you are the managing director of a global corporation.

We all have a unique and interesting story to tell, but are you able to talk about yourself without using your job, achievements or status as an indicator of self-worth? Try it. Next time you are at a social gathering see if you can express your value as a human being without once mentioning what you do for a living or what you are studying. It takes sincerity and honesty. By doing this you are connecting with people on a deeper level because you are actually sharing the real you.

A family that is struggling financially but is highly emotionally intelligent has the resources and skills to cope with the emotional elements of living and will experience a much higher quality of life with both meaning and substance than a family with all the money in the world but with a low level of emotional intelligence.

So ask yourself, how well do you know the people in your life? Do you actually know your friends, children, siblings? What about your partner or your parents?

Your ability to empathise with and understand others is a strong indicator of your emotional intelligence and once you start to see what's inside the people around you, you may realise that there's a lot more going on than is outwardly apparent. Try to put yourself into others' shoes and understand things from their perspective. By doing this, you will begin to experience life and love very differently. What you believe to be right and true can be very different for someone else. Being able to identify and empathise with another is an important part of emotional intelligence and is an integral part of building strong, successful and truly fulfilling relationships.

Relationships are about a true connection that comes from being real and going beyond the surface to explore what lies deep within. Developing strong emotional intelligence and the skills to delve into intimacy and love will provide you with the glue that will enable you to fully connect with others and bind a relationship together lovingly forever.

84

CURRENCY

As you prepare to step into a great, romantic adventure, one thing that you can never have too much of is currency. With plenty of currency you can try all those exciting things, wander off all those beaten paths, while away all those sunny hours – all without worrying how it's going to work out.

And in a relationship, the currency you need is the ability to give yourself emotionally. Money in relationships is easy to figure out – you can see what is fair and right by having a quick look at a spreadsheet. It is also easy to know what you can afford to give and what you are happy to receive – each couple is different depending on their financial circumstances and values. It is easy to look at contributions and be at peace with the figures in black and white. Financial contribution is something you can both calculate.

Emotional input cannot be recorded or calculated so easily. How much are you contributing emotionally and how much is your partner contributing? How much do you need and how much do they need? Have you got the emotional resources to contribute fully or are you emotionally bankrupt while maybe they have worked hard and are emotionally debt free?

You not only need to want a relationship, you need to be ready for one. You would not start a business without capital; it would fail. The same goes for a relationship. You need to have the emotional funds you want to invest, and have some funds to fall back on, just like in business, when you hit hard times.

If you presented a bill for the outstanding amount of $10,000 to be paid by the end of the business day to a bankrupt person their reaction would be one of overwhelming stress. But if you presented the same bill to a person who was debt free and financially secure the reaction to that bill would be completely different.

It is the same with your needs in a relationship. We all have emotional needs to be understood and met and only a partner with 'funds' will be able to meet them without feeling overwhelmed or pressured. Without the funds their empty emotional account will be projected on to you.

Has a partner in a relationship ever said 'I just need some space' or 'You are too intense'? Chances are, he or she was just emotionally broke. Your wishes may have been quite reasonable, but your partner was just unable to meet them.

So when dating and going through the wonderful experience of falling in love, be kind to others and make sure that your 'account' can fully fund this new relationship, and that the person you are investing in is emotionally free of debt with resources available for you. And keep in touch with your intuition. Make sure you are not putting all your funds into a 'business' with no return on your very precious investment - your heart!

EXIT LOUNGE

Suzie

Welcome to Destination Love.

We hope you have thoroughly enjoyed the journey, but before you leave us, a few last thoughts to help you make the best of your time here. (A very, very long time, we hope!)

No two people in the world are the same, so is it any surprise that each couple experiences love and relationships differently? Our past can dictate our expectations, good and bad, and as we get older we can become set in our ways. But without letting go of the past we can't continue to grow.

When you begin a new relationship, remember this is a new chapter of your life. Sometimes memories of the past are hard to let go. Even if your relationship with your ex was not full of wonderful times or what you would want in your life today, it is still familiar – and familiarity feels safe. The unknown can be exciting and new but also incredibly scary. Years of routine, ways of doing things, regular events or traditions can be habitual and comforting, and can give us a feeling of belonging in an otherwise lonely place. But in order to grow both personally and in a relationship, letting go of old patterns and routines is necessary because it allows room for a new chapter to begin and for love to grow within that story.

How far do you think two divorced people will get in a new relationship if they attempt to live the life they had once shared with their previous partners? Living in the same way and with the same routine without changing or adapting is not healthy or fair. Your new partner needs and deserves a new place in time, an open, clear space to be the unique and individual person that they are. You can't change your partner like a pair of socks and expect them to fit into your world like your last partner did.

Love is not about one person slotting into another person's old ways. It is about exploring each other's lives and nurturing the growth of new routines and traditions that are about both of you. Love is about two people coming together and creating their own world, not rehashing an old routine.

Some people try to control their lives with familiar routines because, subconsciously, they think they can also control rejection, disappointment, hurt or failure. The truth is they are not controlling anything; they are being controlled − by FEAR!

"Loneliness remembers what happiness forgets..."

Always trying to stay in control of your life means never allowing yourself to be vulnerable. You can never fully love or be loved without revealing yourself and allowing yourself to be vulnerable. Control is bravado; it is not authentic or real. It is a wall, a façade, a mask hiding a deep fear of letting go, fear of exposing yourself, fear of being free to feel all emotions. Hiding behind a façade creates a false sense of security, only showing the world what appears to be a 'together' person: neat, organised, punctual, emotionally predictable, stable, strong, unflappable... In reality if you don't allow yourself to be open and vulnerable in a relationship, you are quite the opposite. You are afraid.

Now, we are not saying that being diligent, punctual and organised are not great qualities. We are questioning the extremes and the fear that is motivating them. If you are afraid to drop the façade, it is time to ask yourself what it is you are hiding or what you are scared of.

Expecting another person to accept any barriers you have put up around you is not fair. Love does not grow if one or both of you are on that path. You need to be courageous and generous enough with your heart to step out and make a change.

To set yourself free and make yourself available you must take the next step and move out of the safety zone, leaving familiarity behind to create a new loving and fulfilling relationship, a different relationship to what you once had. Letting go is part of life, and letting go of past loves and lives is the only way your new love can bloom.

A HAPPY ENDING

Suzie

So, you have found a partner! You have been busy dating and experiencing life and now you are in a new and exciting relationship! Congratulations! You have both had the 'talk' and decided to be exclusive. That means no more new dates, only dates with each other, your new love!

It may be daunting but the truth is you are now sitting in the roller coaster of love, in the front seat, full of anticipation for what lies ahead. Well, get ready for the ride of your life! But as you go, do everything you can to ensure that this ride never stops. Keep one eye out for some of the warning signs.

Can you relate to this?

You are going to work sleep deprived because you are spending the hours between 7pm and 4am, making passionate love and swapping stories until the wee small hours of the morning. So much to talk about! Finally, someone who listens to your every word, understands your painful past, someone who validates all your feelings of heartache and despair, family dramas and love-life disappointments. You feel exhilarated and on top of the world.

After a while the conversations change and the hours and hours of storytelling come to a halt. Slowly you realise that the butterflies you felt have disappeared, and things have settled to a steady pace, almost routine-like. What has happened? It was a wonderful few months and now all you can feel is a strange shift in the relationship. Your partner seems disinterested or distracted by work, and you no longer share your innermost thoughts and feelings with each other. Something has changed. Something is different.

This point in your relationship is crucial; it's important to understand why. At the beginning it is common for people to only share stories from the past. This is easy because these stories had absolutely nothing to do with your current partner and therefore are not confronting. Although these stories come from the heart they are removed from your current relationship and are only as revealing as you allow them to be. You don't have to give away too much if you don't want to. Talking about the past can bring up interesting reactions, because the past is about another time and place where your new partner feels no accountability. You are communicating on a meaningful level, because you are sharing, but you are sharing your history, not your 'now'.

Think about a story your partner told you that made you feel uncomfortable because it was about a happy time they shared with an ex. Think about how different you feel when it's an unhappy story. Not so bad right? Interesting, because when you think about it, shouldn't your reaction to these stories be the opposite? Shouldn't you be sharing the joy with the happy story and the pain with the sad? You would if it was a friend or relative telling you a similar story. These reactions only reveal that you are human – with fears and insecurities, little voices in your head, wondering about the past, wanting to know but not wanting to know. These feelings can be an indication of how vulnerable you feel in this new relationship. It's hard to imagine these feelings when we are not in a new relationship phase. They seem absurd when we are alone or in a safe, committed relationship, we forget and can't imagine the vulnerable place we once stood in as we began to open our heart to a stranger.

Acknowledging the past is important because it helps us understand each other and support each other in the present, going into the future. But try to put your energy into now, because now is all there is. Yesterday is gone and tomorrow is not promised to us.

One of the ways you may 'hide' yourself from a partner is by presenting yourself as the type of person you think they want to see; agreeing with ideas, movie choices or holiday destinations. But that is not being honest. You're not exactly lying or cheating but you're not being entirely true either. You are simply being agreeable because you are seeking approval. Isn't it important that they fall in love with the real you?

It's hard to open up and let someone in. But the only way to a long and fulfilling relationship is to strip yourself back and share yourself openly and honestly with another person. It's time to reveal the real person inside, time to invest in truth. It's not enough to only physically be there, you have to be emotionally fully present.

The stories you swap and the issues you have shared from your past are no longer enough, your conversation must take a big shift to the present and focus on the story you are creating together now. The story of the two of you and how things are working for you in this relationship.

The big difference between couples that 'function' and couples that 'connect' is what they share within that bond and how.

Couples tend to talk in two ways.

1. **From the head** – thought-out answers, logical, analytical, appropriate responses that sound reasonable and fair. This maintains a distance between individuals which they can hide behind. It allows them never to give themselves fully to the other. It is communication ruled by fear and ego, used by those afraid to be open and to really love.

2. **From the heart** – tapping into your feelings and speaking straight from your heart without censoring. That means without going into your head to think about what you should or shouldn't say. These are your truths and should be treated with gentleness and care by both of you because they come from your most sincere and special place: your heart.

So try to speak from the heart as much and as often as you can. Tap into emotions when you feel joy or pain. Speak them! Just say whatever comes out. Remember, they are only emotions, and are nothing to be frightened of. We are living, breathing beings, not robots, and we have feelings and emotions. Start using the words 'I feel' instead of 'I think'. Remember that this is a unique and special relationship and it is about the heart. Leave the 'I think' line for the office!

Have you ever watched two people get married and noticed that they can't look at each other for more than a few seconds? They are making the promise to spend their lives together but they are afraid of exposing themselves or being really seen by another. They have never been intimate (and we don't mean sex) and yet they are walking down the aisle! Make sure that's not you. Intimacy is a thrilling and life changing experience and definitely worth investigating if it's new to you.

Here's a great exercise that really works.

Stand opposite your partner and hold hands. For no less than three minutes you are going to stand and look into each other, through the windows of the soul - the eyes - without turning away. It may help to put on a beautiful song so you can time this experience. It might also help you feel an added depth of emotion.

As you do this, notice the feelings that run through you as someone looks deep inside you. You may want to laugh, cry, sweat or shake; you may find it so confronting that you want to look away. Please don't. Try to stand and just look into each other's eyes, literally, without looking away. If you begin to laugh, just breathe and come back to where you are. If you feel like crying, let the tears roll down your cheeks, don't look away, keep looking into your partner's eyes.

You have just experienced intimacy. IN-TO-ME-SEE! If you have never done this before it may be overwhelming but it should be beautiful. This is the part of yourself you should be sharing with your partner; this is tapping in and experiencing emotion. You are allowing someone you trust to see inside you and you are looking inside them. There is no superficial world or activity or humour to hide behind as you stand face to face, sharing yourself and truly being seen.

Notice how connected you feel when you talk and look at each other after this exercise. Feel the intimacy. That bond you share with your partner that you do not share with anyone else. After this exercise you will gain new insight into the phrase 'making love', what it feels like and how deeply connected you and your partner become.

When you feel distance coming between you, stand together again, hold hands and reveal yourself to each other. This develops trust that will help your relationship grow to another level, a far more substantial and meaningful level.

When you tap into your heart and begin to fall in love you also open up the vault of life experiences that you may have tried to lock away inside. This is a necessary process. Unless you deal with the hurt and disappointments of your past life, these things have a way of returning, tapping you on the shoulder and saying, 'Remember me?'

Don't be afraid or ashamed of these old wounds. Feel them and heal them. Share them with your trusted partner. It is the only way to truly know one another, grow with one another and experience love and connection.

We all come into a relationship with a history. That can mean we have little triggers that are not necessarily caused by our present partner. It is very important to have the courage and ability to share your innermost feelings when they arise and also the ability to understand and recognise your partner's. That is intimacy. Pretending the pain from the past or triggers from the present do not exist or will simply disappear will not help your relationship develop. You need to work on finding the courage to share yourself and your vulnerabilities with your partner.

Being intimate with another is also about exposing your self, tapping in to your heart and soul and loving from that very special and unique place. It is about being honest, knowing yourself and showing yourself, stripped of all superficialities. It's about who you are, nothing more, nothing less. If you don't know what or who that is, you need to investigate, because that is what you have to offer in a romantic relationship, that is the stuff that counts and that will bring you happiness and fulfilment.

Resentment and boredom can only survive in a superficial relationship where identities come from job descriptions, possessions, or anything that is done to seek approval or validation from one another. These are the people that look outward for fulfilment and happiness, and not inward. The only place you need validation is from yourself. Without depth and layers we are purely 'Teflon-coated' – everything simply slides off. To love and be loved and take your relationship to the next level, to tap into each other's joy and pain and feel it inside, you need to share your innermost thoughts truthfully. Stand tall and be proud to share your beautiful self, and to start loving and living authentically.

Thankyou

Suzie

Special thanks to my beautiful mum Ann I love you with all my heart and I miss you every day...you showed me by example, what love, loyalty, kindness and strength is... I am so proud to be the daughter of the most emotionally intelligent, loving, and honest, open woman I have ever known.

To Clayton Barbeau Thank you for your love, support and wisdom. For seeing who I am, being there for me always, for letting me know you care. You have a permanent and very special place in my heart; you are truly a remarkable man.

To Ben Cooper Thankyou for being the amazing man you are - for sharing the experience of true love with me, for your kindness and unwavering support. You showed me what it feels like to be truly loved and cared for by a man.

Deb

To my wonderful husband Paul Webber Thank you for your love, clarity, patience and unfailing support.

Special thanks to fabulous french champagne and junk food, who were both responsible for getting me through the lean single years.

To my son Geoffrey Thank you for everything?!!??! Well, maybe not the punk phase!.... I love you.

To Leslie Max Heine Thank you for the intro, and for being a bro!

TRUE DATING STORIES

Flatulence

I had been invited to my new boyfriend's house on Sunday night to meet his family. I was excited and nervous and spent some time choosing a pretty dress to impress his parents, knowing only too well the importance of first impressions.

I hired a DVD and ordered take-away Indian curry the night before so I could get my beauty sleep and be fresh for meeting my potential future husband's family. I was giddy with excitement and put the tummy rumbles down to nerves. Shortly after I arrived and had been introduced to John's family, his father thought it might be fun to tell a few jokes to break the ice. Trying to be appreciative, I roared with laughter. Suddenly a loud explosion nearly lifting me from the ground filled the air, followed by a deathly silence. I had broken wind but I couldn't blame the family pet because they didn't have one! The blood rose to my cheeks as the odour permeated through room. Not even the roast in the kitchen stood a chance against the pungent odour. I never heard from him again...

Bye Bye Baby

I met a hunky guy as I was picking up my morning coffee and the attraction was instant. We chatted as we waited in line for our lattes and we exchanged cards. That afternoon he phoned and invited me out for a drink. I could not believe my luck! I thought this only happened in movies! We met for a drink later at a quiet bar. The conversation was electric and we were both on fire. We had an honest chat about life and love. I was incredulous! How lucky for me! I had found this gorgeous single guy. Like a true gentleman, he offered to give me a lift home and things were really heating up as we walked to his car. I hopped in the front, threw my bag in the back seat and was horrified as it bounced off a baby seat.

For the first time my single man was lost for words as he realised he had forgotten to remove the evidence. At that moment it dawned on me he was neither single nor available after all...

Please email us your most memorable dating stories - weird, wonderful, romantic, sad, even hilariously funny. We would love to hear from you... why not share some of your dating adventures with us?

www.ruea.com.au

Lovers Oracle

Heart-Shaped Fortune Telling Cards

by Toni Carmine Salerno

Best-selling artist and author Toni Carmine Salerno's 'Lovers Oracle' has been completely revised and expanded in this new edition of 45 heart-shaped fortune telling cards for lovers and those in search of love. This stunning set, featuring new artwork and expanded and new messages, now also comes with an instructional booklet detailing how to use the cards as well as providing some sample card spreads.

Features 45 heart-shaped cards and instruction booklet, packaged in a hard-cover box set.

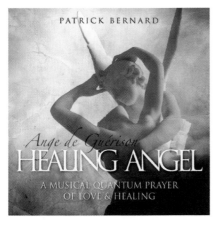

Healing Angel CD

A Musical Quantum Prayer
of Love and Healing

by Patrick Bernard

Containing Angelic Sound Formulas
and invocations, beautiful French
vocals and soothing music, 'Healing Angel' is designed to bring your
body, mind and spirit into an aligned and harmonious state of health and
refresh your spirit.

By absorbing and integrating the powerful invocations contained in this
CD, you will experience the phenomenon of quantum resonance that
constitutes the harmony of the cosmos and restores the body to a state
of health and harmony.

12 Tracks, Total Running Time: 65 mins

For a complete listing of Blue Angel releases, visit our website at:

www.blueangelonline.com

Toni Carmine Salerno Art Prints

Printed on fine textured art papers.

To view the complete range of art prints, visit:

www.tonicarminesalerno.com

Notes

BLUE ANGEL
PUBLISHING

www.blueangelonline.com

Illuminating Hearts and Minds